# Born to Be

# SUPER

## Unleash Your Inner Superpower

P. Madeline Berry

Parakletos
Publishers

First edition
ISBN 978-1-958879-01-6 (paperback)
ISBN 978-1-958879-02-3 (hardback)
ISBN 978-1-958879-009-9 (ebook)

This book was professionally typeset by Parakletos Publishers.
Find out more at parakletospublishers.com

Parakletos
Publishers

# Table of Contents

Introduction ............................................7

What's a Superpower? ..................................15

Superpower ID ...........................................25

Superpower Bootcamp .................................41

Your Truest Identity ...................................51

Protecting Your Identity ..............................61

Sidekicks Are for Winners ............................69

Here Come the Villains................................79

What's in Your Utility Belt? .........................91

Using Your Superpower to Change the World ...........101

Going from Impossible to I'm Possible .....................113

What's Next? ...........................................121

Notes ....................................................123

## Dedication

*This book is dedicated to the first superhero I met in person.
I love you, Mom.*

*Acknowledgments*

*All praises go to the Author and Finisher of my faith, Jesus
Christ. Thank you, Lord.*

*Sunny Kang, thanks for leading the Fivefold Author group.
Your guidance and insight helped me immensely. We finished!*

*Fivefold Authors, you inspire me. Thank you for your incredible
stories. The world will read your books and be changed forever.*

*Dunamis Leadership Team, thank you for being sensitive to the
call of God on the lives of the people you shepherd.*

*Every person, everywhere, you inspire me to see beyond what
you show me. You were born to be super, and I am going to love
watching you unleash your inner superpowers to make the world
a better place.*

# *Introduction*

**Supers (Man-made vs. Natural)**

Superheroes have always had a special place in my heart. From sitting in front of the TV every Saturday morning in the '70s and '80s to watching current full-length movies in theaters, I'm still a lover of superheroes. I remember being eight or nine years old and wishing there was a way to pause the TV every Friday night, so I wouldn't miss *Wonder Woman* while we were at Friday night prayer meetings. Thank God for reruns and, eventually, VHS players!

Like most superhero lovers, I have my favorites. And no one can change my mind about the superiority of my two favorite natural superheroes. You may wonder, "What's the difference between natural and man-made heroes?" I'm glad you asked!

## What Is a Man-Made Superhero?

Most man-made superheroes are regular people who experienced some type of tragic accident that altered their perspective, physical makeup, or abilities. Here are some of the heroes in this category:

- Batman – His parents were murdered, and he used his inherited billions and technology to make tools and become the protector of his city.
- Spider-Man – He was bitten by a radioactive spider, and the venom altered his DNA, giving him spider-like traits.
- Hulk – A scientific experiment exposed him to extreme levels of gamma radiation. When he is angry, he becomes a super-strong, green, hulking beast.
- Iron Man – He was a brilliant inventor/scientist who built a suit that he uses to protect others.
- Captain America – He was a scrawny man who wanted to serve his country and volunteered to be injected with a super-soldier serum to be accepted into military service.

The circumstances surrounding each of these heroes' making caused them to alter their personas. Each was given a superhero name that described their traits, abilities, or influences. Typically, their physical enhancements were amplifications of preexisting aspects of their personalities or tangential actions based on life's encounters.

Take Captain America as an example. Steve Rogers was a frail, sickly man who wanted to serve his country in World War II. Because of his sickly appearance and many physical challenges, the Army would not accept him. Character-wise, he was committed, persistent, dedicated, resilient, and wouldn't take no for an answer. Those natural character traits qualified him to be a candidate for the super-soldier serum. The serum changed his physical appearance, but he was still the same committed, persistent, dedicated, and resilient man. The man he was inside finally matched the super-soldier he became on the outside.

## What Is a Natural Superhero?

Natural superheroes are the ones who were born with all their superpowers. These heroes are ordinary kids who had to go to school and learn like everyone else. The difference is that they were also taught about their gifts and trained on how and when to use them. They were told that they were unique and different from their peers. Here are some of the heroes in this category:

- Superman
- Wonder Woman
- Neo (*The Matrix*)
- The Incredibles (and the heroes in their movie)

Let's look at Superman. Born on a planet called Krypton and named Kal-El, he was sent to earth before the destruction of his home planet and was the sole survivor of his kind. He was an orphan who was blessed to land on the property of a childless couple with a lot of love to give. His parents knew he was special, but I don't think they knew the extent of his abilities. As they found out how different he was, they did their best to put a solid foundation of good, basic principles in him. It's almost like they were following the proverb that says, "Train up a child in the way he should go, and when he is old, he will not depart from it."[1] He had challenges like any kid growing up, but eventually accepted the responsibilities of his special gifts and used them to fight crime and help others.

The thing about Superman is that on earth, his natural Kryptonian bloodline made him capable of super strength and abilities naturally. He didn't have to do anything to be super. He was born with it. He had to dress down to fit in with society. I will admit that glasses and a hairstyle weren't the greatest disguises, but for the sake of the story, it was enough to blend in and not be recognizable. His name was Clark Kent, but he was a super man to his core.

Now, here's my disclaimer: Everything I tell you about my man-made vs. natural hero theory is my own opinion. There is no research backing it, nor will any "expert" acknowledge it. It comes from my observations of the traits and nature of different depictions of heroes.

So how do you relate to man-made or natural heroes? Have you noticed traits in common with either or both types of heroes?

What if I told you that there is another type of superhero I didn't mention? This type of hero doesn't have to hide their identity or put on a mask. Some of them work undercover, hiding in plain sight and doing heroic things without making a big fuss about it. These are the kinds of heroes that have always existed. They are the God kind.

---

1 Proverbs 22:6 NKJV.

If you don't believe in God, that's OK. If you don't believe God makes heroes, that's OK too. It is an unchangeable truth found in 2 Corinthians 5:17, which reads, "Now, if anyone is enfolded into Christ, he has become an entirely new person. All that is related to the old order has vanished. Behold, everything is fresh and new" (TPT). An excerpt of the note accompanying this verse is, "We are not reformed or simply refurbished, we are made completely new by our union with Christ and the indwelling of the Holy Spirit." This is who emerged when Jesus was baptized by John the Baptist.

The likeness of Superman's story to that of Jesus Christ is obvious to me, but I'll give you a few similarities so you can see it too.

- He was born from above.[2]
- His father sent him to Earth to protect humanity.[3]
- He lived among everyday people.
- He didn't abuse his powers.
- He did things no one else did.[4]
- He loved people.

There are also differences in the comparison between Superman and Jesus. Superman was a one-off. He couldn't duplicate himself. Jesus was sent as a model of what humanity could be. He demonstrated the life of a Spirit-filled Son of God living on earth. He even showed that death wasn't the end of life. While He was living, He chose certain people to witness His life. These were His disciples, those who, after Jesus was crucified, became like Him. He left them

2 John 3:13.
3 John 3:16.
4 John 20:30–31.

a blueprint that taught them how to live like Him, and they duplicated His example by converting many others into God-made superheroes. As far as heroes go, Jesus is my all-time favorite.

Again, I define natural superheroes as people who were born with natural gifts, talents, and abilities that didn't have to be learned. I have news for you today: you are a natural superhero! I hear you saying, "Who, me?" I answer you with a confident, "Yes, you!" You were born with at least one innate ability. I call that your superpower, and in this book my desire is to help you identify, exercise, and apply it, every day of your life. The great news is that if you identify as a Christ-follower (aka Christian), God has added another level of supernatural abilities to you.

If this is hard for you to believe, I get it. You may be saying, "There's nothing super about me, and I've been a Christian my whole life!" or "Hero-shmero, I don't believe you!" or best of all, "Tell me more!" These thoughts won't make me back down; they excite me. You ARE a superhero who has been lulled into thinking you're regular, that there's nothing special about you, and that you should keep living an average life like everybody else. It's time to wake up to who you really are. Here's a verse that alludes to your status: "Our lives now represent the one event every creature anticipates with held breath, standing on tiptoe as it were to witness the unveiling of the sons of God. Can you hear the drum roll?"[5]

---

5 Romans 8:19 Mirror Bible.

You are super, and the world is waiting for you to show up. In the coming chapters, I hope to help you transform your thinking and show you how to walk in your superhero traits.

## Power Up

I am your biggest cheerleader. If no one else has ever believed in you, "Hi, my name is Madeline, and I have your back." You are an incredible person, and I cannot wait to show you how amazing you truly are. Are you ready? Let's go!

# Notes

# Chapter 1
## What's a Superpower?

Merriam-Webster defines a superpower in several ways. When referring to people, it is "a power or ability (such as the ability to become invisible or to fly) of the kind possessed by superheroes: a superhuman power."

People are diverse and have common traits, abilities, and specialties. Most of us are doing things we were taught to do versus the thing or things that we do because it's who we are. Many of us are proficient in many things, but have you ever thought about why so many people didn't return to work after the global pandemic of 2020? How many people were asking for a break because they were tired of performing underwhelming, routine actions? How many people do you know who really enjoy their jobs? Why is it that so many people are unhappy with their lives and work? All these questions are rhetorical, but think about how you would answer them if they weren't.

A friend I met in college is a brilliant writer. Her journalism major included writing, and she was good at all forms, but she shines as a creative storyteller. I would have never known that she was such a brilliant writer until she shared a poem she had written after the sudden death of a loved one. I was so moved that I couldn't stop rereading it. Every time I read it, I would shake my head in disbelief that these words flowed out of her in a single sitting. Every so often when I was in a bookstore I would pick up a journal and send it to her to encourage her to express herself in writing.

Her superpower was no longer a secret to me. I recognized it immediately, and I don't know if she hadn't acknowledged it yet. I KNEW the world needed to read something she wrote so they could see what I saw, feel what I felt, and know what I knew about this incredible author. She went on to graduate and was one of the people in the small percentage who used their degree in the field where it was intended. She was amazing at her job. She met and worked with incredible people and accomplished a lot, but every so often I still picked up a journal and sent it to her to remind her about the superpower she was not using. I am still awed by her inconceivable talent. The great news is that she recently published her first book. I have it in multiple formats, and it is a solid read. I celebrate the first in what I hope is the beginning of a long list of literary works that she produces.

I shared that story to demonstrate what happens in most people's lives. Do you know how you can be friends with someone for years and not know something they do in secret that's so good it blows your mind? I think we all have a "something" we do that we share with only a few. I know people whose singing voices are so pure; they can bring you tears. Yet I'm one of only a few people who know they have that ability. The same is true for people I know who have talents that have life-changing potential. Do you know what's crazy? They don't think they are as good as they are! What "thing" have you always done that you haven't shared with the people around you? That one thing could be your superpower!

### Pause for Reflection

If you were out of work during the global pandemic, what did you do with the extra time?

_____

_____

................................................

................................................

................................................

If you were out of work, did you return to your old job role or did you start a new one? Was it in the same field of interest? Would you rather be doing something else? If so, what?

_____

_____

................................................

# Born to Be Super

The point I am making here is that the person sitting in the next cubicle, across the table, or next to you on the couch is possibly one of the most talented people you'll ever meet, but you wouldn't know it because his/her secret superpower will remain secret if you don't engage him/her to have a conversation. One of my goals in writing this book is to help us get to know each other better. We live in a mind-your-own-business world. We don't know our neighbors and barely have true friends. If you are people with the superpower of loving and engaging others, now is your time to flex your super strength. The world needs you to bring your neighbors from behind their closed doors and into the streets to mingle. We are better together than we are apart.

Have you figured out my definition of superpower yet? I'll keep going and share a nutshell version of the story about the fictional computer hacker named Neo. Some people knew him formally as Mr. Thomas Anderson. He was a gifted computer programmer who worked at a leading technology company. He also had a thriving side hustle of creating programs for demanding clientele. If you looked at him, you wouldn't know that Neo had a secret passion, a deep desire to meet a legendary man named Morpheus and discover what the Matrix was. Neo didn't know that while he was searching for Morpheus, a team of people who worked with Morpheus was searching for him.

One night he was continuing his search and was given a lead to find Morpheus. Like true seekers, he followed the lead and within days found himself face-to-face with the legendary icon. The answer to all his questions was found in a single choice: a red pill or a blue pill. By choosing the red pill, his life would never be the same. The blue pill would erase the whole encounter, and he would wake up with his alarm blaring like every other day. His one choice revealed a truth he didn't suspect: he was a superhero. He had to go through rigorous training and near-death experiences, but by the end of the movie, he took flight. Ultimately, he became Superman for his time, saving people who chose freedom and fighting for people who didn't want to yield to a system that drained the life out of people.

Neo's story is an example of a person who was attracted to a superpower he didn't know he had. Some of us are walking around just like Neo. There are ideas or concepts we've had an interest in but never explored. What if you took 30 minutes a day to research that topic to find out why it has eluded you all these years? What if it's looking for you too, and by starting your search, you will attract it to yourself? What if what you find will change your life and everything you've ever known? What if it reveals your superpower to yourself and the rest of the world? The world is waiting for you, and no one will change it the way you will.

*Pause for Reflection*
Take some time to dream. List some topics you want to know more about (one per line). Beside each, write a question you want to research about it.

_____

_____

_____

_____

_____

_____

So, what is a superpower? I define it as the thing(s) that live at the core of who you are. Your superpower may not seem spectacular to you, but when exercised in the right environment, can change the course of your life and others with little to no effort. It comes from the core of your nature. You do it naturally and mostly without thinking. So, what is your superpower? Maybe it's one of these things:

| | | |
|---|---|---|
| Acting | Doctoring | Planning |
| Administrating | Dreaming | Problem solving |
| Art | Engineering | Psychoanalyzing |
| Athletics | Exploring | Selling |
| Building | Gaming | Singing/Rapping |
| Coding | Generosity | Speaking |
| Compassion | Hope | Storytelling |
| Composing | Humor | Teaching |
| Dancing | Inventing | Traveling |
| Designing | Organizing | Writing |
| DJ-ing | Parenting | Zoo keeping |

These are examples, but there are so many more. What is yours?

You may be saying, "Madeline, I don't have a clue what my superpower is." If that's you, my enthusiastic response is, "Let me help you discover it!" But before we get started, I want to remind you of a Bible verse I mentioned earlier: 2 Corinthians 5:17. The moment you identified with Christ's birth, life, death, resurrection, and ascension, you were transformed into His image. You became a brand-new, super being that has never existed before. You moved beyond human and became a new species of being. That verse from The Passion Translation (TPT) reads, "Now, if anyone is enfolded into Christ, he has become an entirely new person. All that is related to the old order has vanished. Behold, everything is fresh and new." You can now do the same things Jesus did and even more. That alone makes you a superhero with superhuman abilities like invisibility, transportation, supernatural authority, bi-locationality, the ability to shift matter, levitation, telepathy, and so much more. Have you tried walking on water or through a wall lately? I'll talk more about this in chapter 10. Don't skip ahead! (If you're ready to expand your mind, I recommend you read a book by Justin Paul Abraham, *Beyond Human*. Another great read is *Limitless* by Nancy Coen.)

**Power Up**

We're living in a time when people have said "no" to going to jobs to do things they hate. A lot of those people don't quite know what they're supposed to be doing, but they know they are not meant to be running on a hamster wheel waiting for a check every two weeks. If you are one of those people, will you let me help you find your superpower? It's somewhere inside of you, waiting to be discovered and honed to change you and the world around you.

Let's go get it!

# Notes

# Notes

# Chapter 2
## Superpower ID

Identifying your superpower requires honesty, introspection, and the help of candid people in your circle of friends, family, coworkers, and community. It's likely that you already know what your superpower is. It may be buried under years of repetitious routines you did to make ends meet. It could be waiting for you at a place you once used as a personal retreat from the noise of your life. It could be connected to a hobby you started doing to relax at the end of a long week. The point I'm making is you have probably been exercising your superpower your whole life, and because it's a part of your nature, you haven't recognized it as something viable that makes you super or gives you a platform for a career.

I feel like I need to take a moment to encourage you with a Bible verse that helps me when I'm freaking out because it seems like something is missing from my life. Have you felt that way? It's like accomplishing something amazing and wondering what's next. Or being overwhelmed because the path forward is hazy with average options and you were made to be extraordinary. An excerpt of 2 Peter 1:3 says, "Everything we could ever need for life and godliness has already been deposited in us by his divine power."[6] A long time ago, I read a book called The Law of Recognition by Mike Murdock. The summation of this law is that everything you will ever need is somewhere around you, waiting for you to recognize it. I believe that with my whole heart, and I have all confidence that you already have what you need to go on this exploratory journey with me to recognize and embrace your superpower.

**Kids' Stuff**

Let's talk about your growing-up years. Who was your childhood hero? If you were like me, you had a lot of them. My number one heroine was, and still is, my mom. She's my own version of a real Wonder Woman. As the youngest of her five children, I watched as she exemplified the virtuous woman described in Proverbs 31:10–31. She is a woman of great faith, and through all manner of circumstances she (and God) raised us to love God and people. As I think about what her superpower is, I am torn by myriad choices. She's got it going on and continues to amaze me with her tenacity and zeal for life. She has used the gift of partnering with Christ to step into one of her superpowers of loving people well. She is awesome at it too!

---

6 2 Peter 1:3 TPT.

So, who was your childhood hero? Who was the person whom you stopped and stared at when they walked into the room or when you saw them on TV or at church or school? What about them was so captivating that they made you want to be like them? What were those traits or characteristics? Take a break from reading and think about that. If you need more than a moment, take the time you need. Are any of those characteristics or traits on display in your life? Why or why not?

## Pause for Reflection

Use this space to talk about your childhood hero or heroes. Answer the questions about the traits and characteristics that made them heroic to you. Do you think you display any of those traits or characteristics today?

_____

_____

_____

_____

_____

_____

_____

_____

_____

_____

............................................

I realize that we've all had different growing-up experiences. I don't want you to compare my experiences with yours. I want you to examine what you have learned, what decisions you made, how your worldview was shaped, and who you have become as a result of your time as a child. You may have challenges looking back because of bad memories. However, I encourage you to ask God to take you on a journey through your childhood. During that journey, ask Him to show you where He was whenever the times were toughest. Trust me when I say, "He's been with you every day of your life, whether you felt Him or not." A portion of Hebrews 13:5 AMP reads, "for He has said, 'I will never [under any circumstances] desert you [nor give you up nor leave you without support, nor will I in any degree leave you helpless], nor will I forsake or let you down or relax My hold on you. . . !'"

You may be asking, "Madeline, why is this necessary?" The reason is that as a child, your heart is pure and full of hope. You can see things you want to be in others and make early choices/decisions to be that way when you grow up. I think my sisters would agree that what we saw lived out in front of us through our mom is the foundation of who we are today. When we look at our grown-up lives, there are strong indicators that we were shaped in her image and likeness with a deep love for God and others.

The same is true for us as children of God. In Matthew 18, Jesus' disciples asked Him about who is the greatest in heaven's realm. "Jesus called a little one to his side and said to them, 'Learn this well: Unless you dramatically change your way of thinking and become teachable like a little child, you will never be able to enter in. Whoever continually humbles himself to become like this little child is the greatest one in heaven's kingdom realm.'"[7]

Youthful expectation is something we're all born with. Unfortunately, some experiences and circumstances can turn off the hope switch inside of kids at early ages. Thankfully, God is constantly partnering with people to redeem and restore broken things. If you had a rough childhood and can't put yourself in a place of youthful expectation and hope, consider praying and seeking counsel. Asking for help is a responsible thing to do when you realize your past is holding you back from moving forward into your future.

*Pause for Reflection*

Writing/journaling is a proven means of expressing memories, thoughts, plans, hopes, dreams, ideas, and more. If you need some space to review some things that may have come up in your mind when reading the last section, start expressing them here. If you run out of space, consider purchasing a notebook or a journal to continue these thoughts. (Please remember, this is your personal journey to unleashing your superpower. No one else has to read this copy of your book and your personal thoughts.)

---

7 Matthew 18:3–4 TPT.

_____

_____

_____

_____

_____

...............................................

...............................................

...............................................

## School Days

Were you a lover of school, or not so much? I loved learning in general, so school wasn't hard for me. I had fun throughout most of my formal educational years. Do you know that your superpower may be connected to your favorite school subject? It could also be connected to the thing you got in trouble for doing most while you should have been learning. If we were doing senior superlatives, what type of adult would your high school classmates say you were most likely to do/be? Think about that and who you are today; did your classmates guess right?

Did you have one of those assignments in middle school when you made predictions about where you would be and what you'd be doing in the future? We did one when I was in 7th grade. Maybe your parents were like my mom; she kept some of our old school projects. I still have the list of things preteen Madeline predicted. I knew things about myself then that are still true now. One of the items referenced computers. It was one of the things I was right about. The timing for the prediction was spot on! I think you get my point. If you can tap into who you have been for as long as you can remember, you may be able to identify parts of your superpower. While I was in high school, I started creating graphic flyers and banners. The seed of graphic design was planted; and for a portion of my life, I owned and operated a graphic design company. I even worked as a computer consultant for some years after that.

There's a thread that is interwoven throughout your life. If you take some time to think back to conversations from past times with different people, you may see it. I don't know what yours is, but I know there is one. You may be the creative carpenter who shows up to build something as an outlet or a way to relax from a busy week. You may be the author who has been journaling at the beginning and end of every day to express herself in words and to get heavy things off her mind. You may be the runner who wakes up at the crack of dawn to run before the rest of the world begins to spin around him. You may be the budding chef who watches cooking shows and tries to duplicate dishes in the kitchen after work. Whatever the thread is, it likely encircles something that has been present for as long as you've been alive. Focus on the freedom you feel when you're doing it. Your superpower flows from a place of freedom and joy.

### Pause for Reflection

Think back to your schooling experiences. What was your favorite subject? Is what you do for a living connected to your favorite subject? Did your high school

classmates deem you one of the class superlatives? Who/
what were you most likely to be/do?

_____

_____

_____

_____

_____

_____

## University of What's Next

What did you do after high school? Some take the college
route, and others choose to take a break and work or travel. I
think either choice is a good one if you're learning. College is
a breeding ground for many things, but I believe it's the place
where teenagers go to learn responsibility. Parents push their
almost-adult babies out of the nest and trust the many years
of home training to serve as foundations for their adulthood.
College kids become responsible for managing their own
schedules, finances, time, and relationships. It can be a time
of exploration and identity, as well as a place to discover
innate superpowers.

I sprinted to get out of the house after high school. Home
life wasn't bad; it was the small town in North Carolina
where I grew up. After seeing the same people for 13 years, I
wanted to see some different faces, increase the variety of
things I could do on a Friday night, and move out of small-
town America. I only applied to out-of-state schools. If I saw
my high school classmates again, it would be at the reunions.

I knew the world was bigger than my surroundings, and I wanted to see more of it. Traveling is one of the things I love most in my life. Even 7th grade Madeline knew I wouldn't be living in North Carolina as an adult.

## Adulting

After college, there are several options. Some choose an extension of college in pursuit of advanced and professional degrees. Others accept positions in exciting new careers, while others settle for something that pays the bills. Still, others end up back home because they can't find a job in their field of study. The tragedy in this entire educational journey is that no one helped them find out what their superpower is and how to use it.

There are rare cases when the young adult stumbled over his superpower and chose to change his major after three years of chasing a degree he didn't enjoy. Despite being cut off by his parents, he got a job to pay his own way while learning to hone his abilities. He worked a full-time job while taking classes as he could afford to pay for them. It took him another four years, but the struggle wasn't a problem for him. He had found the joy of being super. His pursuit was refocused, pointed, and direct. He lived off minimal hours of sleep between working and school. He had something to believe in: himself. By the time he graduated, he had created a community-based project that helped thousands across the city with several options to expand it across the country.

Sadly, that wasn't my story. I earned my degree in engineering while experiencing college life. By the end of my five years as an undergrad, I resisted the college comfort zone and rejected the offer of pursuing an advanced degree. Some said I was crazy for turning down the invitation to another degree, but I was burned out on classroom learning. I wanted more. I learned a lot about myself and the nature of people in general while choosing to work in various roles at my alma mater. I built on my natural gift of graphic design and fell in love with entrepreneurship. I was a mentee of an incredible woman with a work ethic like nothing I had ever seen. All my experiences after college added to my abilities. I became knowledgeable about countless things, but I hadn't found my superpower yet.

## The School without Walls

The truth about every person you meet is that there are layers of experiences inside of them. The face you see every day is possibly a work face or church face, or even an acquaintance's face. From the day we are born, we are constantly learning or collecting data. Our subconscious mind makes decisions about our experiences and encounters, our likes and dislikes, what we will accept or reject, and how we react to external stimuli. These things begin to build inside of us to form our view of the world we live in and the people we do life with. Sometimes we encounter situations that cause us to make promises to ourselves about loving others or what we allow as acceptable treatment from others.

Studies show that by the age of five, children have a sense of self-esteem that tends to remain relatively stable across their lifetimes.[8] Starting with parents or guardians, each of us has been impacted by external influences since the day we were born. Depending on how you perceived your surroundings and the people who had the power to influence your life, your outlook on life reflects the sum of the information you received about yourself.

Think about your parents, other close relatives, siblings, family friends, church influences, friends from school, teachers, bosses, significant others, mentors, children, counselors, and all the people who have had a voice in your life. Consider encounters with these people and how things they have said impacted your life. As you look in the mirror, you see a representation of people's concepts, opinions, and ideas about yourself that you have agreed with. This could be good or not so good.

The point I'm making is that like most adults worldwide, we are tightly wound around an idea of who we are. I am asking you to unwind all the layers to find out who you truly are at your core. I've gone through that process and have faced up to many messed up ideologies, images, and characterizations about myself that were deeply rooted. There is a natural gift inside of you that could likely be buried under years of lies you have believed about yourself. The sad truth is that there is only a small group of people who care to see that part of you. I am one of those people, and I'm here to believe with you through your self-discovery process. My promise to

---

8 Molly McElroy, "Children's Self-Esteem Already Established by Age 5, New Study Finds," UW News, November 2, 2015, https://www.washington.edu/news/2015/11/02/childrens-self-esteem-already-established-by-age-5-new-study-finds/.

you is to love you as God loves me. I take that very seriously. There is nothing you have done or will do to make you unlovable. You need to know that.

*Pause for Reflection*
Answer these questions:

1. What are you naturally good at doing? (List as many things as you want.)

   _____

   _____

   _____

   ...................................................

2. Having lived your life this long, think back to your childhood with your adult knowledge and finish this sentence, "when I grow up I want to be a(n) _____. (List as many things as you can remember.)

   _____

   _____

   _____

   ...................................................

3. Are you currently participating in any of the things you listed above? If so, which ones? If not, why not?

_____

_____

_____

4. If money wasn't an issue and you couldn't fail, how would you spend your days?

_____

_____

_____

5. Ask about five (5) of your friends/family/coworkers/ managers/pastor what they think your strengths are. Record their answers here.

_____

_____

_____

_____

_____

6. Consider your answers to all the questions above. What would you say is (are) your superpower(s)?

_____

_____

7. How can you integrate your superpower into your life as a regular, daily activity?

_____

_____

_____

## Power Up

It's not too late to discover your superpower. It may be hidden under a heap of worries, fears, doubts, tragedies, victories, or struggles. It's there, waiting for your attention. There is a spark of joy that you may feel when you're doing something random in your day. You likely ignore it and go about your day as usual. I challenge you to recall it, engage it, explore it and believe in it. The world needs what you have. Don't be stingy, sharing is caring!

# Notes

# Notes

# Chapter 3
## Superpower Bootcamp

Do you know what your superpower is yet? If you haven't discovered it, don't worry or feel rushed or put it under a timeline. The world has been waiting this long, so what are a few more days, weeks, or months? I believe that since this is something you're seeking, you are destined to find it—sooner rather than later. Read Matthew 7:7–8.[9]

Think back to Neo from *The Matrix*. (If you've never watched *The Matrix*, I encourage you to stop reading this book and watch it now. No, seriously. Go and watch it.)

---

9 "Ask, and the gift is yours. Seek, and you'll discover. Knock, and the door will be opened for you. For every persistent one will get what he asks for. Every persistent seeker will discover what he longs for. And everyone who knocks persistently will one day find an open door." Matthew 7:7-8 TPT

His character was introduced as a regular guy by day and a hacker on the dark web by night. We saw him at home running unending searches on his computer. Do you know what he was looking for? He was looking for someone to answer his question, "What is the Matrix?" What he didn't know is that the same person he was looking for was simultaneously looking for him. Have you heard the Chinese proverb that says, "When the student is ready, the teacher will appear?" I learned that the full quote actually says, "When the student is ready the teacher will appear. When the student is truly ready . . . the teacher will disappear."[10] Wow, right?

Finally, Neo got a lead to the answer to his question. He followed breadcrumbs that lead him to Trinity. She confirmed the question and provided an opportunity to bring him face-to-face with the person he's been looking for. Unfortunately, the meeting wasn't at the same place, and the next day, he was still searching. Another delay! As if that wasn't frustrating enough, suddenly, he's questioned by people who were also looking for the same person, and somehow they wanted Neo to lead them to him.

Have you been there? You are searching for something, and after a long and arduous search, you finally get a breakthrough. You get a piece of information that could be a dead end, or it may be a clue that leads to a deeper search. Either way, you're the same person, just with another piece of possibly useless information. If that's where you are, I have a

---

10 Attributed to Lao Tzu, the Chinese philosopher best known as the author of Tao Te Ching.

question for you: "How badly do you want it?" Here's another question: "What's the harm in opening one more door?"

Neo was on the road to meeting Morpheus, the man he had been searching for his whole life, and someone in the car offended him. He had a choice to make. The car has stopped, and the ultimatum has been presented. "It's our way or the highway!" With one leg out of the door, he didn't want to take someone else's path because he was tired of being a follower; he wanted to make his own path. Trinity stepped in and reminded him of the futility of rejecting the single action that could be the doorway he always wanted. If we could have heard his heart, it was probably beating out of his chest at that moment.

What are you searching for? Are you ready to sit and learn? If you have an idea of what your superpower is, then it's time to focus and start developing it. Along the way, you may be offended by something you see or hear or are asked to do. You have a choice to make. I once heard someone say, "Some of the deepest truths you'll ever learn come in offensive packaging." Are you willing to look past the offense to unpack the treasure you're seeking?

You're probably asking, "What do I do to develop my superpower?" That's a brilliant question, and I'm glad you asked. Develop, by definition, is
   1. to bring out the capabilities or possibilities of
   2. to cause to grow or expand
   3. to elaborate or expand in detail
   4. to bring into being or activity

5. to grow into a more mature or advanced state
6. to be disclosed; become evident or manifest

You're probably still looking at these words and thinking, "HOW? How do I develop my superpower?" I encourage you to keep asking questions because that's how you get answers. Have you ever asked a hard question that no one could answer, but as you're driving along or reading a book or having a random conversation with friends, your answer comes through the radio or the book or the conversation? Remember the law of recognition I mentioned in chapter 2? All the answers to your questions are already in your life simply waiting to be recognized. The journey to developing your superpower may begin with a single question. Here are some questions you can ask yourself:

1. Who do I know with a similar superpower? (List as many as you want.)

_____

_____

........................................................................................

2. Are there books about it? List them and start reading or listening.

_____

_____

........................................................................................

3. Are there videos, movies, websites, or tutorials that focus on the details of my superpower?

_____

_____

4. Are there discussion groups or online forums I can join?

_____

_____

5. What steps can I take to activate my superpower?

_____

_____

_____

It's time to go into research mode. You are about to interview yourself. Some of the questions may be hard to answer, but I encourage you to take this process seriously. The results are worth it if you're willing to do the work.

Neo met Morpheus, and the life he once knew became a memory. That last door he walked through changed him forever. His teacher appeared because he was ready. He opened his eyes and walked with his own legs for the first time. The beautiful part was that there was an entire community of people surrounding him and helping him to develop and train. He was immersed in a whole new world.

(Cue the music to "A Whole New World" from Disney's Aladdin movie.)

## Check-in Time

So, how are you doing? Do you take time to gauge where you are in your current moment? If you are squinting in confusion while you're reading this, it's likely that you don't have this practice. Some people are calling it mindfulness. Others call it meditation. I call it checking in. At my day job, I schedule check-in calls with all my customers. These calls do at least two things:

1. Inform the customer where they are from our perspective.
2. Allow the customer to correct our perspective by providing us with their opinion of where they truly are.

The bonus thing these calls can do is show both sides how we can align on plans to meet a project's deadline. We can set meaningful goals to talk again to see how we're progressing and troubleshoot anything that may become blockers to completion. We get to partner on the best solutions that produce win-win scenarios for each side.

Now it's your turn. Take a few minutes and do an internal check-in. Fill in the blanks. Take as much space as you need.

1. How am I doing with this discovery process? Am I feeling good, frustrated, bordering on giving up, needing a little more discovery time, or something else?

_____

_____

_____

2. Am I becoming more self-aware?

_____

_____

_____

3. Have I identified my superpower? Am I overthinking it?

_____

_____

_____

4. Do I have the resources I need to start developing my superpower?

_____

_____

_____

5. How much time am I willing to invest in developing myself and my superpower?

_____

_____

_____

.................................................

Spend as much time as you need on the answers to these questions. Another thing you can do is identify people you trust to tell you the truth. Survey them by asking them what they think your strongest gifts are. When you're finished, let's talk about your identity. I'll meet you in the next chapter when you're ready.

**Power Up**

Have you ever watched a movie where people are treasure hunters? They follow clue after clue after clue. Somewhere along the line, there's an opportunity for them to quit. As they are walking out on the dream, they look once more and notice something they hadn't seen before. It was a book that was out of place on the shelf or a feature on the wall that looked like it could move a different way. They try one last time, and a secret door opens to the hidden treasure.

Life is like that. There is a treasure hidden inside of you that you must find to live the life you were meant to live. If you have acknowledged that God exists and sent Jesus to live an exemplary life for us to follow, you're one step closer to finding your hidden treasure. 2 Corinthians 4:7 reminds us, "We are like common clay jars that carry this glorious treasure within, so that this immeasurable power will be seen as God's not ours." The best part about this is that God doesn't have a problem sharing the spotlight with us because that's why He made us . . . to be like Him.

Many people fail to find their hidden treasure and settle for the mundane existence that passes as a responsible life. The risk and time it takes to find the treasure don't seem worth it. I recently heard a story of a man who wanted to start his own business. He put it off, got married, and had kids. Plus there were a lot of responsibilities that his job was sustaining. He didn't take the risk. His dream of becoming an entrepreneur was what he remembered when he was lying on his deathbed. He told his son about it, and the thought stuck with his son when he was faced with the same desire. The son didn't want to have the same testimony of not trying like his dad had, so he took the risk to start a business. Today, he is a successful serial entrepreneur and teacher who helps other people succeed.

# Notes

# Chapter 4
## Your Truest Identity

I believe identity is the most critical thing in our lives. How you see yourself is the foundation of your worldview. Who do you think you are? In Genesis 1:26–27 we get a picture of who we are: "Then God said, 'Let us make mankind in our image, in our likeness, so that they may rule over the fish in the sea and the birds in the sky, over the livestock and all the wild animals, and over all the creatures that move along the ground.' So God created mankind in His own image, in the image of God he created them; male and female he created them."

These verses set a tone—a foundation for us as created beings. The problem is that most people don't realize the value of being created to be like and look like the Creator of all things. Who and how is this invisible Creator? What is the image, and what is the likeness? All these are great questions. Indulge me while I delve into the who and how of this great Creator.

Let's start with another section of scripture that describes creation at the same point of reference: the beginning. John 1:1 from the Mirror Bible says, "To go back to the very beginning, is to find the Word already present there; face to face with God. The one mirrors the other. The Word is I am; God's eloquence echoes and concludes in him. The Word equals God."[11]

John 1:14 continues, "Suddenly the invisible, eternal Word takes on visible form—the Incarnation, on display in a flesh and blood Person, as in a mirror. In him, and now confirmed in us. The most accurate tangible exhibit of God's eternal thought finds expression in human life. The Word became a human being; we are his address; he resides in us. He captivates our gaze. The glory we see there is not a religious replica; he is the authentic begotten Son. The glory that returns in fullness. Only grace can communicate truth in such complete context."[12]

If you haven't realized it yet, these passages in John are referring to Jesus. Colossians 1:15 says it a little more clearly: "In him the image and likeness of God is made visible in human form in order that everyone may recognize their true origin in him. He is the firstborn of every creature." Am I saying that you look like Jesus? Well, yeah, I am saying that!

---

11  Mirror Bible. Emphasis added by the author.
12  Mirror Bible. Emphasis added by the author.

Every person ever born on earth was created in the image and likeness of God. That includes you.

Before you shrug me off, I have something else to tell you. Are you ready? The Messiah was prophesied throughout the Old Testament. When He arrived and began His ministry, He repeatedly said that if you saw Him, you saw the Father. That statement was blasphemous to most everyone who heard it because they thought it incredulous that he would say that He looked like God. Take a deep breath and read this . . . YOU LOOK LIKE THE FATHER TOO!!!

Go to your nearest mirror, look into your own eyes, and say these words: "I LOOK LIKE GOD!" Say it as many times as you need to get used to hearing it. Even if you are a seasoned believer, please do this exercise. Faith comes by hearing, and sometimes you need to declare things aloud so that you hear yourself. Knowing and accepting the truth that you are made in the image of God can change your entire perspective on life. We are the only creatures who bear the image of God and who have the same creative ability that He displayed in the beginning.

That covers the "image" part of your identity. Now, let's talk about the "likeness" part.
- What is God like? We know He's the Creator of everything. Does that mean you are a creator too? Yes, it does. Humans are the most creative beings in existence.
- How did God create? He used words.

- o Genesis 1:3 says, "And then God announced: 'Let there be light,' and light burst forth!"[13]
- o 1:6: "And God said, 'Let there be a dome between the waters to separate the water above from the waters below.'"
- o 1:9: "And God said, 'Let the water beneath the sky be gathered into one place, and let the dry ground appear.' And so it happened."
- o 1:11: "Then God said, 'Let the land burst forth with growth: plants that bear seeds of their own kind, and every variety of fruit tree, each with power to multiply from its own seed.' And so it happened."
- o 1:14–15: "And God said, 'Let there be bright lights to shine in space to bathe the earth with their light. Let them serve as signs to separate the day from night, and signify the days, seasons, and years.' And so it happened."

Do you get the picture here? God said something and everything He said manifested. We are just like Him! You may not believe me, but your natural superpower is driven by your tongue. I'm imagining the look on your face; you don't believe me? Challenge accepted!

Look around you. You built the room you're sitting in with your words. That furniture, the paint on the walls, the flooring, the lighting, what you're wearing, the food you ate earlier, and everything else you see around you. The most powerful part of this observation is whether you like what

---

13 All passages from Genesis 1 are quoted from TPT.

you see or not, you have the superpower of Creation in your mouth!

Sometimes I think a warning should come with this ability to create. The reason is because it works regardless of what you say. It can be good or bad. The power of your gift of creation is that every word that comes out of your mouth will manifest. Just imagine what things would be like if God changed His words at the beginning to, "Wow, it's dark out here!" We would be living in a vastly different creation or maybe not at all.

A good example of this is Job from the Bible. Job was a righteous man who worried too much about his kids. He knew they liked to party and have a good time. His biggest worry was that in their celebrations, they may have offended God and sinned. Job 1:5 reads, "When these celebrations ended—sometimes after several days—Job would purify his children. He would get up early in the morning and offer a burnt offering for each of them. For Job said to himself, "Perhaps my children have sinned and have cursed God in their hearts." This was Job's regular practice.[14] Job repeatedly worried aloud about his children. They all died suddenly, and in Job 3:25, he said, "What I always feared has happened to me. What I dreaded has come true."[15] Do you see the power of words? The point of this short story, as I understand it, is that Job spoke and acted in fear, and the very thing he kept declaring and sacrificing against manifested. (Note to

---

14 Job 1:5 NLT. Emphasis added by the author.
15 Job 3:25 NLT. Emphasis added by the author.

theologians: please don't contact me about my interpretation. I'm not available to discuss it with you.)

The bottom line is you are an environment builder. Your words are the building blocks of what you see around you. Your identity is founded on the words that have built you. If your parents built you with words that empowered you and confirmed your ability to do anything you put your mind to, you are probably a very successful person. Those words were likely confirmed by the people who surrounded you growing up. Their words built you into the person you are. As you look at your reflection in the mirror, take a moment to realize that every word spoken over you, that was received as truth, formed you.

The reverse is also true. If you were surrounded by negative words and associated images, your perspective on life is probably pessimistic. You may not see the glass as half full. You may not expect the best outcomes from situations you're in. You may think you are forgettable and have little worth. People's words did that, and you agreed with the words. Don't worry, this is not a death sentence. Now that you know how words work, you can start to reframe yourself and your environment.

Take some time and think about your earliest memory of words that had a negative effect on your life. Write down the opposite of those words and begin to repeat the positive confession over your life. Do this every time you remember something someone said to you that made you feel devalued. Here's something you can say to yourself every day. It comes from 1 Peter 2:9, "You are proof of the authentic generation; you give testimony to the original idea of the royalty of true priesthood; you are a perfect prototype of the mass of the human race. You are the generation of people who exhibit the conclusion of the prophetic, poetic thought of God that has come full circle. You publish the excellence of his elevation and display that your authentic identity has been rescued out of obscurity and brought into his spectacular light."[16]

## *Pause for Reflection*

What words have you become? Think of how you define yourself when you say things like: "You know me ..." or "That's just me ..." or "You know how I am ..." What words framed you? Ask your family, friends, coworkers, and others who love you to describe you in three words or less. Explore the words and determine if that's really who you are or if that's who you are to them. There is a difference!

_____

_____

_____

_____

_____

_____

_____

_____

_____

16 Mirror Bible. Emphasis added by the author.

**Power Up**

You are a beautifully made masterpiece of God's creation. In your own time, read Psalm 139:13–18. Ponder the vastness of creation and the fact that God is aware and concerned about every aspect of you and your life. Your identity is founded in Him. Knowing who and how He is defines who and how you are. Make no mistake, you are phenomenal. If there has ever been a time to see yourself for who you really are, take a moment to wrap your arms around yourself and give yourself a hug. Tell yourself this truth: "I was made in the image and likeness of God. He has made me His address. I am complete in Him. I look like God. I act like God. I AM is in me."

# Notes

# Notes

# Chapter 5
## Protecting Your Identity

In the last chapter, I explained the foundation of your identity. If you're still not sure about who you are, please reread the chapter as many times as it takes to be comfortable in knowing who you are without any doubt.

This chapter is about protecting your identity. All superheroes have regular names they use in everyday life. These are some examples:

| Regular Name | Hero Name |
| --- | --- |
| Clark Kent | Superman |
| Diana Prince | Wonder Woman |
| Thomas Anderson | Neo/The One |
| Peter Parker | Spider-Man |
| David Banner | The Hulk |
| Bruce Wayne | Batman |

Unless you were closely connected to these "regular" people, you wouldn't know they were superheroes. They protected their hero identities to the best of their abilities. One day while thinking about this topic, I wondered why protecting their hero name was such a big deal. In my opinion, it was love. They wanted to protect their loved ones from being kidnapped, hurt, or threatened by their enemies. They knew their loved ones were weak points in their armor. In many cases, they relinquished the desire to be married to protect the ones they loved from undue danger.

For you, protecting your identity doesn't have to look like this. You are a vessel of love who lives your life in faith. The Bible says, "Fear cannot co-exist in this love realm. The perfect love union that we are talking about expels fear. Fear holds on to an expectation of crisis and judgment and interprets it as due punishment. It echoes torment and only registers in someone who does not yet recognize the completeness of their love union."[17] Instead of fearing retaliation from your enemies, you are protecting the knowledge of your identity against all the negative voices that are trying to make you forget who you are. You are a superhero with creativity as your foundational superpower. In the words of Queen Ramonda, King T'Challah's mother (in Black Panther), "Remember who you are!"

There are an onslaught of voices in our daily environments that are presenting alternatives to your righteous character. Don't get me wrong, distractions happen any time you set yourself on a course to do better in life.

---

17  1 John 4:18 Mirror Bible.

Whether you are getting fit, changing your diet, writing a book, reading more, spending less money, rebuilding your credit, or something else, the opposition will arise to challenge your resolve to change old habits.

Remember the day you were fasting, and your coworkers came to your desk to treat you to lunch? They had NEVER invited you to lunch AND offered to pay, but today they were moved to have lunch with you. How about the time you were changing your schedule to add prayer time, and the phone that hadn't rung all day began to ring? What about the lesson God placed on your heart to begin studying? It seems like just when you got through the first chapter, something happened with your spouse, child, or other family member or friend that you had to focus on at the exact time you had set time aside to study. Those are called distractions, and if you allow them, they can cause you to lose focus on your identity.

Remembering who you are and protecting that knowledge is a 24/7/365 job. We are constantly being bombarded by TV shows, news, social media, negative people, and others who are attempting to dictate what is "scheduled" to happen in our lives. Whether you accept or reject what "they" say is up to you. Remember that what you accept today will eventually become a part of what you see around you in the future. When "they" say we are in a recession, I challenge you to remember the image and likeness of your Creator. You can agree with "them" and declare recession in your life, or you can do what God did in the beginning. Just like He declared light in the darkness, you can declare abundance where "they" are projecting lack or shortage. "They" are calling for sickness; you can declare divine health. "They" are showing you negative news that could make you cynical and sad. You must focus on the good things that are all around you because you've been creating positive surroundings. Be grateful. Gratitude will change your negatives to positives in no time. You must combat the environment "they" are projecting with positive expectations of your future surroundings.

Protecting your identity also means building relationships with people who are in alignment with the core of your identity. Do they know who they are? Are they pursuing better things in their lives? Are they able to encourage you when you don't feel super? Do you do the same for them when they need encouragement? One of my favorite Bible verses about friendship is Proverbs 27:17, "As iron sharpens iron, so one man sharpens [and influences] another [through discussion]."[18] Translation: having good friends means being accountable and helping each other when necessary. It also means being responsible, trustworthy, honorable, honest, and of good character.

Remember chapter 4, when I demonstrated how God created by speaking? I didn't go through the entire first chapter of Genesis, but there's one thing He did that you need to be comfortable doing. After He made something, He observed His work and appreciated its beauty. For example, Genesis 1:4 says, "And God saw the light as pleasing and beautiful."[19] Again, the end of Genesis 1:10 says, "And God

---

18 Proverbs 27:17 AMP.
19 All passages from Genesis 1 are quoted from TPT.

saw the beauty of his creation, and he was very pleased." He did this repeatedly, enjoying the process of expressing His creativity.

Like Him, you have permission to review your creations (books, music, art, dance, clothes, computer code, blueprints, engineering designs, etc.) and admit that you did a good job. You are also permitted to receive compliments from others when they acknowledge the beauty of your creations or the amazingness of your superpower. You are like your Father, the Creator of all things. Genesis 1:31 says, "God surveyed all he had made and said, 'I love it!' For it pleased him greatly. . . ." He loved the products of His superpower, and He announced it aloud. He wasn't shy and falsely humble. He showed confident assurance that what He was doing was magnificent.

When He created us, He announced His idea and made it happen. To quote Genesis 1:26–27, "Then God said, 'Let us make a man and a woman in our image to be like us. Let them reign over the fish of the sea, the birds of the air, the livestock, over the creatures that creep along the ground, and over the wild animals.' So God created man and woman and shaped them with his image inside them. In his own beautiful image, he created his masterpiece. Yes, male and female he created them."

**Power Up**

YOU ARE LIKE YOUR FATHER! (Yes, I am shouting at you.) Protect your identity with every fiber of your being. You are a unique, custom-created masterpiece, made in the image and likeness of God to change the world with your power to create. Use your words to create your world. Read Proverbs 4. The entire chapter is life-giving, but if you need to focus on a few verses, start at 20 and read through 27:

"Listen carefully, my dear child, to everything that I teach you, and pay attention to all that I have to say. Fill your thoughts with my words until they penetrate deep into your spirit. Then, as you unwrap my words, they will impart true life and radiant health into the core of your being. So above all, guard the affections of your heart, for they affect all that you are. Pay attention to the welfare of your innermost being, for from there flows the wellspring of life. Avoid dishonest speech and pretentious words. Be free from using perverse words no matter what! Set your gaze on the path before you. With fixed purpose, looking straight ahead, ignore life's distractions. Watch where you're going! Stick to the path of truth, and the road will be safe and smooth before you. Don't allow yourself to be sidetracked for even a moment or take the detour that leads to darkness."[20]

*Pause for Reflection*

Use this space to describe who you are. You can also write any thoughts that were running through your mind as you read this chapter.

_____

_____

_____

_____

---

20 Proverbs 4:20–24 TPT.

# Notes

# Notes

# Chapter 6
## Sidekicks Are for Winners

What do we say about sidekicks? To most people, a sidekick is the second person mentioned after the main member of a superhero duo. I think the most popular is the Dynamic Duo of Batman and Robin. Here's the key to understanding any hero + sidekick relationship: both are heroes who can stand alone but are smart enough to trust the power of unity. For this writing, I want you to consider Neo and Trinity as a powerful pair of superheroes, another dynamic duo. (Side note: If you still haven't watched *The Matrix* yet, please stop reading right now and watch it.)

Sidekicks have been portrayed as the less capable or the less dominant member of the hero partnership. The truth is that dynamic duos help each other. Trinity found the Matrix before Neo. She was instrumental in helping him make several decisions that changed his life. Remember when she hacked into his computer and told him to follow the white rabbit? She orchestrated their meeting so he would have a person to connect to the hacker on the other end of his computer. Remember how close Neo was to getting out of that car when they wanted to check him for bugs? It was Trinity who reminded him about the mundanity of his life in the Matrix when she said, "You already know what's down that road." If he had ignored her, he wouldn't have met his teacher, Morpheus.

Trinity believed in him before he believed in himself. Do you know why she believed? She had received a prophetic word from the Oracle. She held on to that word while helping to reveal Neo's true identity to himself and everyone around him. She was clutch[21] in moments when no one else could speak his language. Their relationship empowered their success—because they believed in the power of unity.

What was Neo's part? Neo was a learning machine. I believe that Tank's chair hadn't fulfilled its purpose until Neo sat in it. He knew he didn't know as much as the people training him. He worked with Tank for countless hours to learn everything that was available. He was a machine! He learned so much that he thought he could do anything, but with knowledge comes testing. After one session he said, "I know Kung Fu." Morpheus' reply was, "Show me." He demonstrated his knowledge, but there was still more to learn.

---

21 Clutch: "The ability to perform well on a certain activity at a particular moment, despite external pressures, influences, or distractions." https://www.urbandictionary.com/define.php?term=Clutch.

That's where Trinity came in. Inside the Matrix, Neo wanted to do things on his own and in his own power. He didn't want to put someone else at risk of losing their life. Trinity wasn't having any of that. She understood the power of teamwork and unity. Morpheus needed to be rescued or all of Zion would perish. Trinity was not about to allow Neo to carry all the weight of being the hero in saving their friends in Zion. They collaborated and operated as a single unit, each knowing what the other needed without being told. They brought their whole selves to the task and yielded to the strongest gift when it was needed. Neo needed someone who could fly a helicopter. Trinity got the download and jumped in the pilot's seat. They played off each other's gifts without needing to be the leader. Neo recognized and embraced the fact that he was a part of a team. Each team member knew how to lead when it was their turn, just like all the members knew how to step back and follow to allow the appointed leader to lead.

Have you ever been in a team-building exercise where you learn more about the people you're working with? It's incredible how learning the strength of your teammates empowers the group. It all boils down to building and growing relationships. Finding yourself partnered with someone whose superpower is complimentary to yours is a recipe for success. Think about the Super Friends, the Justice League, the Avengers, or the Guardians of the Galaxy. Think about winning sports teams, humanitarian organizations, and community outreach efforts. It's like a symphonic performance where every instrument is in perfect harmony, melody, and rhythm. When there's a solo, the rest of the orchestra reduces its volume to provide background support. When the solo is over, every instrument's volume equalizes.

The power of unity is unbeatable. The strongest thing on earth is a group of people working together towards the same goal. Have you ever read about Babel in the Bible? Check it out when you have a moment. It's found in Genesis 11:1–9. In verse 5, God looks at what the people have accomplished so far and said, "If they have begun this as one people sharing a common language, then nothing they plan to do will be impossible for them."[22]

Do you remember the power God demonstrated at Creation? Everything He said appeared in front of Him. Now think about what He said about the people at Babel. If we think about what He said, we come to realize that He defined the power of unity. Words that come to mind when I think about Babel are synergy, collaboration, teamwork, and unity. These are the same words I think of when I think about heroes, sidekicks, and their teams. If we team up to work towards a common goal and operate as a single unit, nothing can stop us. How incredible would it be if we lived in unity with everyone? Imagine that!

I have the privilege of being a partner of World Vision, a global Christian humanitarian organization whose mission statement is, "We partner with children, families, and their communities to reach their full potential by tackling the causes of poverty and injustice." I have been partnered with

---

22 Genesis 11:5 TPT.

them for a long time, adopting and supporting children and their communities in various parts of the world.

One day at the beginning of 2008, I woke up wanting to run a marathon. As someone who had never run track or done any long-distance running, I knew this was a God-inspired idea, something He could empower me through. Internally, I asked, "Where do I start?" Days later, I received an email from World Vision that said something like, "Help us dig wells in Africa by running the Chicago Marathon with us!" I knew this answered my internal question and I signed up immediately. They provided the conditioning and pre-training schedules on how I could become a marathoner in roughly 10 months. It was grueling and required my dedication and commitment. Every early morning long run on the weekend, I would talk to God and remind myself of different scriptures like, "I can do all things through Christ who strengthens me" (Philippians 4:13); "But they that wait upon the Lord shall renew their strength . . . they shall run, and not be weary, and they shall walk, and not faint" (Isaiah 40:31); and "My grace is all you need. My power works best in weakness" (2 Corinthians 12:9).[23]

When I showed up in Chicago for marathon weekend, I realized that all my efforts were matched by hundreds of others from around the world. We were Team World Vision! We gathered to pray before the race began. All the training and endurance workouts were about to pay off. But wait, I forgot to tell you that I was raising money too! Truthfully, I was never running alone. I wasn't a hero operating alone; I

---

23 2 Corinthians 12:9 TPT.

had my family, friends, financial supporters, and a radical team of heroes running with me. As we ran, millions of people lined the streets and called out our names to cheer us on. I thought of the Cloud of Witnesses mentioned in Hebrews 12. This event changed my life. That year is one of the most impactful years I've ever lived. World Vision and 109 other charities raised over $9 million to change the world in a single day.

Here's a final example. Have you ever watched the Disney/Pixar movie The Incredibles? (As you can see, I like cartoons too. If you haven't seen it, go watch it.) Mr. Incredible, aka Bob Parr, was adamant about working alone. His biggest fan, Incrediboy, kept showing up to help him defeat the criminal elements he was pursuing. Incrediboy, aka Buddy, was a genius inventor and wanted to be Mr. Incredible's sidekick. He was repeatedly rejected. I'll fast forward through the government mandating the heroes to retire and get regular jobs. Bob married Elastigirl and started a family of supers. Bob was bored and out of shape when along came an opportunity for him to come out of retirement and start doing secret hero work again. He jumped at the opportunity and learned that Incrediboy had become Syndrome, a supervillain who wanted to send an invincible AI robot to attack the city. He had the controls for the robot and hoped to emerge as the greatest hero of all time by defeating the robot and saving the city. The problem was that he didn't care how many people got hurt in the process, and the robot was constantly learning how to protect itself. In the end, the entire Incredibles family had to work together as a team to defeat the robot and Syndrome. Instead of a single sidekick, Mr. Incredible had four team members who could be ready to fight crime at a moment's notice.

If you are a Christ follower, you are a part of His body. Whether you are new to the Body of Christ or a seasoned believer, you are called to serve a significant role in life. Guess what? You are still called to greatness even if you are not a Christ follower. Indulge me while I share Ephesians 4:15–16: "Instead, we will speak the truth in love, growing in every way more and more like Christ, who is the head of his body, the church. He makes the whole body fit together perfectly. As each part does its own special work, it helps the other parts grow, so that the whole body is healthy and growing and full of love."[24] You read that correctly, Jesus Christ believes in teamwork! He does not mind having eight billion sidekicks on earth, of which you are one.

*Pause for Reflection*

Do you have a sidekick? As you are considering what your superpower is, who comes to mind when you think of partnering with someone else? Write any other thoughts that popped in your mind while reading this chapter.

---

24 Ephesians 4:15–16 NLT. Emphasis added by the author.

_____

_____

_____

_____

_____

_____

_____

**Power Up**

You are a superhero who can easily stand alone and do incredible things in the world around you. You can also be a sidekick to someone else to help with their mission. You are surrounded by super others who may be able to partner with you to make a duo. Or there may be a team of heroes already working together that is looking for another to add to their strength, skillset, and exposure. You don't have to work alone. The power of unity can change the world. Teaming up is not a failure or an affront to the idea of being a superhero. It's a sign of wisdom, strength, and trust in the power of unity.

Note: To learn more about World Vision, visit https://www.worldvision.org/.

# Notes

# Notes

# Chapter 7
## Here Come the Villains

By now you should have figured out that I believe you were super since the day you were conceived. Nothing tragic or life-altering had to happen for you to gain your powers. The simple miracle process of childbirth afforded you the title of champion. Of the average 40 million sperm vying to get to the egg, you succeeded. If your mom had a challenging pregnancy, you had to fight a little harder to survive gestation, and around nine months later, the champ was born. Go you!!

No superhero story is complete without identifying the villain, the nemesis, the bad guy, or whatever name you want to call the person who is in constant opposition against the hero. If you think of a hero, it's easy to identify the villain.

Here are some examples:

| Hero | Main Villain |
| --- | --- |
| Superman | Lex Luthor |
| Batman | Joker |
| Spider-Man | Dr. Octopus |
| Thor | Loki |
| Avengers | Thanos |
| Fantastic Four | Dr. Doom |
| Neo | Smith |
| Captain America | the Red Skull |

The thing about villains is that they don't have to be people. A villain could be an environment, a system, a mindset, a tradition, a trauma, or many other possibilities. My definition of a villain is anything that challenges your identity and attempts to make you prove you are who you say you are. I believe one of our greatest villains is our thoughts. You may be wondering how these things could be villains in our lives. Let me demonstrate with an example.

I know of a woman whose greatest superpower is public speaking, storytelling, and encouraging others. She is a dynamic leader of two global organizations. She is a wife, mother, daughter, friend, author, teacher, mentor, and so many other things. I believe she has impacted people on every inhabited continent. I heard her tell her story about how she was born and abandoned in a hospital without a name. She was adopted into a family where she was sexually abused for several years of her life. Because of her nationality, she was considered a minority in the community where she grew up. When it was time for her to step into leadership, people told her she was not qualified. Think about the number of villains she overcame to become the woman she is today.

Her villains:
1. Abandonment
2. Rejection
3. Sexual/emotional abuse
4. Shame, Guilt, Unworthiness
5. Memories

She was surrounded by people who told her how insignificant she was. She was constantly battling shame, guilt, unworthiness, unsuitable, being identified as a female minority, and many other conditions. In my opinion, her greatest villain was and still is the battle in her mind. Thankfully, she is equipped to defeat these villains by confessing God's truth about herself daily.

Can you relate? Take a moment and think about your life. How did you come to be who you are? How has your environment shaped your daily reality? What systems were you subjected to while growing up that can still trigger memories of conditions you were exposed to? What villains have you defeated in your life and what did you learn about yourself in the process? What motivates you to get out of bed every day?

*Pause for Reflection*
Take some time to think about your life. Answer the questions from the preceding paragraph.

_____

_____

_____

_____

_____

_____

.................................................................................................

The mind is a part of the soul. Your soul comprises your mind, will, emotions, and intellect. It's programmed by the things we see, hear, learn, and participate in throughout life. If, after years of doing something the same way, you decide to change it, your soul will reject the new thing because it is unfamiliar and not proven. It wants to avoid danger and protect you from hurt and is often connected to deep fears of failure. Addictions occur because your soul enjoys the results of habits we form over time. If the habit is like smoking, your soul's addiction to it will cause you to stand in freezing temperatures to satisfy its desire for nicotine. Other things have the same addictive spin.

Merriam-Webster defines addiction as "a compulsive, chronic, physiological, or psychological need for a habit-forming substance, behavior, or activity having harmful physical, psychological, or social effects and typically causing well-defined symptoms (such as anxiety, irritability, tremors, or nausea) upon withdrawal or abstinence."[25]

---

25  https://www.merriam-webster.com/dictionary/addiction

There are countless resources about addictions and how they work. In most instances, we address addictions in negative contexts. Did you know you can have positive addictions too? Go to a gym or workout facility, and you will see people who are addicted to exercising. Do you have a friend who always has a book in his/her hand? They are addicted to reading. How many gamers do you know? Do you know what they are addicted to? My point here is that addictions come in all forms. The soul includes things we've learned, so changing our perceptions of how words are defined can be the first step to defeating this villain.

The soul is the reason why many people have issues with change. In many ways, your soul is lazy. It doesn't want to take hard routes or submit to painful processes when your present condition is easy and painless. The comfort zone is like a utopia created by your soul. It's where all your favorite creature comforts live. The soul is the barrier you face when you want to modify your eating or exercise more. The good thing about your soul is that it is trainable. It is said that you can make or break a habit in 21 days. This is a soul-training technique that requires commitment, discipline, and willpower. This is also how to defeat the villain that is your soul. Another soul-training technique is your ability to recreate your world. Start with something small and use your words to retrain your soul.

People who survived the Great Depression and lived through the 2008 financial crisis have memories of losing everything. Their souls were scarred by the pain of having all their wealth and financial security stripped from them overnight. How do you think those people view their finances now? Many are penny pinchers who find value in every stray coin they see discarded on the ground. Even through good economic climates, they scrimp and save every dime, stuffing money under mattresses or burying it in their backyards. The common song of their souls is, "I will never trust anyone else with my money."

People who served in the armed forces and had to face deployments in war zones had natural villains, but the most damaging villains live in their minds. The things they saw and had to do reshaped them. I have heard family members recount that the loved ones who left were not the same when they returned. They were exposed to conditions and environments that reshaped them. Some came home missing limbs, and many came home missing the ability to reconnect with their families and communities. (Note: If you served abroad in the armed services in volatile conditions, I'm praying for you. I honor you as one of the heroes who put your life on the line to protect the liberties I enjoy daily. Thank you for your service!)

What about real people who oppose you? The next villains are people who don't like you or what you stand for or are attempting to accomplish. In today's terms, we would call people like these "haters." I used to teach a course to young entrepreneurs. One of the things we told them was that leaders are rare. Out of 100 people, 87 would be followers, ten would be haters, and three would be leaders. We were teaching three-percenters and the possibility of them encountering a hater in their life was a sure thing.

What do you do about a villain who has found a reason to dislike or oppose you? That is a great question! This is where you lean to your natural superpower of creativity, and into the example Jesus left for us. Have you ever read what Jesus said in Matthew 5? Check out how verses 43 through 48 read from The Message: "You're familiar with the old written law, 'Love your friend,' and its unwritten companion, 'Hate your enemy.' I'm challenging that. I'm telling you to love your enemies. Let them bring out the best in you, not the worst. When someone gives you a hard time, respond with the supple moves of prayer, for then you are working out of your true selves, your God-created selves. This is what God does. He gives His best—the sun to warm and the rain to nourish—to everyone, regardless: the good and bad, the nice and nasty. If all you do is love the lovable, do you expect a bonus? Anybody can do that. If you simply say hello to those who greet you, do you expect a medal? Any run-of-the-mill sinner does that. In a word, what I'm saying is, Grow up. You're kingdom subjects. Now live like it. Live out your God-created identity. Live generously and graciously toward others, the way God lives toward you."

Wow, right? Villains need love too. Who knows why they don't like you? The better question is this: are you mature enough to see past their hostile actions against you and respond with love and kindness? That takes super strength and a whole lot of prayer. I believe you can do it. There's no victory in going tit for tat against someone opposing your forward progress because that is a waste of time and a distraction from your work.

I remember having a coworker who was my elder. She always treated me differently than she treated others. I often heard her making sarcastic remarks about me when I was leaving the room. Thankfully, I was in Christ and wanted to live and work in peace with my colleagues. I prayed and asked God how to bring peace into the relationship. I noticed that she liked a certain type of music. I found out who her favorite artist was and purchased the latest copy of their music to give to her. When I gave it to her, she was surprised and genuinely thanked me. Her attitude changed toward me from that point. She later retired, and after a few years, I saw her at a mall with her grandchildren. She was genuinely happy to see me. It was as if that single gift erased years of negative feelings and rewrote our relationship with good memories. Dr. Martin Luther King, Jr. said it best: "Love is the only force capable of transforming an enemy into a friend."

If you're dealing with villains, try one of these ideas:
1. **Ask for Help:** Tap into your creativity and ask God for ideas to resolve the difference. You will be surprised how quickly you will receive an answer. Be sure to keep your eyes and ears open for solutions when you ask questions. God speaks in many ways. Remember the law of recognition because the answer is closer than you think.
2. **Giving:** Have you ever tried giving a gift to someone who doesn't like you? Giving is a powerful tool to diffuse an attack from someone coming against you.

Receiving gifts, especially unexpected gifts, is a heart-opener that can transform an enemy into a friend. Try it.

3. **Grace:** Grace is when you get what you don't deserve. Think about it: you are a recipient of grace every day. Remember that, and give those haters some grace too. Do they deserve it? Probably not, but neither did you. Pay it forward because they may grow into a better version of themselves and need a little grace-filled space.

4. **Mercy:** Mercy is when you don't get what you deserve. God's mercy is why I'm alive today. If you take some time to think about it, you probably have the same testimony. The biggest example I've ever seen of mercy is when Jesus was hanging on a cross and said, "Father, forgive them; they don't know what they are doing."[26] I know this is a hard example to follow, but I promise that if you get used to forgiving people and then praying for them, you will mature more and more.

5. **The Love of God:** Besides creativity, love is God's most dominant superpower. I could write an entire volume of books about the love of God. It's the gift that keeps on giving. He gave everything He had as a demonstration of His love for you, me, and everyone else in the world. (Read John 3:16.) Know this: people who need love are some of the hardest people to love. Many of your biggest villains have never known unconditional love. I dare you to become an agent of God's love and unleash it on your toughest opponent! As you do that, keep this truth as a foundation in your

26 Luke 23:34a MSG

mind and heart: God loves every person you will ever meet as much as He loves Jesus. That includes your villains.

There are more ways to combat villains, but let's stop here. Your discipline in dealing with enemies is a yardstick for measuring your growth. Don't be afraid to ask for help when you are your worst villain. You can do this! Don't take it from me; listen to Jesus from John 16:33: "I have spoken these things to you that in me you will know the sweet and assured resonance of my peace. In the world you encounter extreme stressful times, but be of good courage, I have conquered the world-order."[27]

## *Pause for Reflection*

While you've been reading this section, have you thought about villains in your life? Take some time to list them and the ways you can defeat them.

_____

_____

_____

_____

_____

_____

_____

_____

---

27 John 16:33 Mirror Bible.

**Power Up**

You are a natural-born champion. Though champions are loved by many, some people oppose them in various ways. As you have grown up, your biggest supporter or villain has been your environment. The people who have been adding information to your soul, the things you've watched or learned from the people around you, and the actions that have developed into habits are all a part of a system that can either work for you or against you. Now that you know you have the power to be someone different, will you exercise that power to become the best superhero you can be? The world is still waiting for you to change it. Start with yourself and keep going. You've got this, Champ!

# Notes

# Chapter 8
## What's in Your Utility Belt?

What can we say about the utility belt? I think Batman wore the most famous utility belt. It held different tools he could use to aid him in fighting criminals. As he has developed, so has his utility belt. His Bat family also were known for wearing utility belts of their own. I smiled while researching the different tools Batman kept in his belt. There were batarangs, a batline, bolas, smoke pellets, tracers, concussion mines, and myriad other Bat tools. He always seemed to have the exact tool needed for his situation.

Batman and his crew were in the minority as far as wearing utility belts. That doesn't mean other heroes didn't have additional tools to help them. Wonder Woman kept the Lasso of Truth on her belt, she wore bullet-proof bracelets, and her headband could be used as a boomerang. Iron Man's suit was packed with tools to help him blast past his opponents. Spiderman always had another shot of webbing to disable the criminal he was fighting. Every Guardians of the Galaxy member had something tucked away in a pocket to throw at something when they needed it. Even Superman used his arsenal of natural abilities to combat the evil he was facing.

What's the point? The point is, as a superhero from birth, you have a collection of tools you can use to overcome whatever is in front of you. You don't need a physical belt to remind you of the tools you have to defeat any villain; however, since you may be stepping into your superhero status, allow me to help you define some of the things in your arsenal. This list is not exhaustive, but I believe it's enough to get you started.

*Creativity:* You can create your way out of any circumstance, situation, or face-off in front of you. Remember that you were created in the image and likeness of the Creator of all things. He demonstrated how to use creativity when He spoke the world into existence. "The Lord merely spoke, and the heavens were created. He breathed the word, and all the stars were born. He assigned the sea its boundaries and locked the oceans in vast reservoirs."[28] Remember: you are like God.

*Holy Spirit:* If you have made Jesus Christ the Lord and the chief example for your life, you have full access to His Spirit. The Holy Spirit is a Person and an equal part of the

---

28  Psalm 33:6–7 NLT.

Holy Trinity. Holy Spirit is your advocate, teacher, leader, helper, and guide. He leads you to the truth. He is everywhere you are. If you ask for help in the face of a villainous situation, He will answer you with strategy. He will make you look smarter than you are, by giving you ideas, inventions, and insight into all sorts of things.

Good news: If you haven't made Jesus Christ the Lord and chief example for your life, you can do that at any time by acknowledging that He is the Son of God and that He lived, died, and was resurrected. It's that simple. Check out Romans 10:9–10.

Also, good news: If you don't want to make Jesus Christ the Lord and chief example for your life right now, you're still covered and super. God loves you whether you love Him back or not. He promised through a prophet named Joel, "I will pour out my Spirit upon all people. . . ." Read Joel 2:28 and Acts 2:17. Whether you know it or not, every person on the planet is being soaked in the glory of God. What is this glory? Glory has many definitions to me. One of them is Heaven's atmosphere filled with God's presence and power. Right now, you are immersed in it. If you randomly get ideas for how to help groups of people, that's the glory of God, and you're covered in it. Keep doing things that will help others, and whether you like it or not, you're exemplifying Godlike tendencies.

*Fruit of the Spirit:* The beautiful thing about the Holy Spirit is that He comes with a fruit basket or a full utility belt. Tucked securely in this basket is the undefeated power of love. Love is a world-changing tool loaded with its own tools. There's joy, peace, patience, kindness, goodness, faithfulness, gentleness, and self-control.[29] I would love to go into more detail about these tools, but I want you to make learning about these things an exercise you do with the Holy Spirit. Ask Him to show you how each of these things can work as tools in your super life. You will be glad you did!

*Compassion:* What is compassion doing in my belt? It's a fact that we've needed someone to show us compassion at some point in our lives. Showing compassion can be a miracle-generating act. In Webster's Dictionary 1828, one of the definitions says, "compassion is a mixed portion, compounded of love and sorrow."[30] Compassion is like reaching out and helping someone who needs a head start or a hand up out of their situation.

When I finished college, I didn't have any prospects for employment. I was out of options when a woman who worked at my alma mater reached out to me to ask if I would like to work with her in a temporary position. She was also an alumna and needed some help on a special project being conducted from one of the vice presidents' offices. I didn't know what I would be doing, but I jumped at the opportunity. Fifteen years and multiple job titles later, I resigned to move across the country and chase my dreams. She was one of the smartest, most hardworking women I've ever known in my life. She had compassion for me and

---

29  Read Galatians 5:22–23. (Any translation will do.)
30  https://webstersdictionary1828.com/Dictionary/compassion

opened a door to a career that I never imagined. The memory of her life and work ethic are still alive in me.

I am compelled by compassion when I think of what was done for me. I believe everyone can be moved by compassion to act on behalf of others. Have you ever read the Bible story about Jesus feeding the 5,000? Read about this in Mark 6:30–44. The miracle of multiplication happened because Jesus was moved by compassion for the crowd of hungry people. You may be moved by compassion for someone who needs help somewhere in your superhero life. Don't turn away. Make space for the miracle-making potential of showing compassion to someone who needs it.

*Faith:* Faith is a force. Most people hear the word and think about a religious practice or belief. Do you know that you use faith continuously in your daily life? I guess you want to know how. Every day when you wake up, if you had active use of your limbs when you went to sleep, you have faith that they will work when you get up. If your bills are paid, you have faith that your lights will work when you flip the switch; that your water will come out of the faucet when you turn the knob; and that your Wi-Fi will connect your computer and mobile devices to the Internet. If you have a car, you get inside and turn it on, full of faith that it will work as well as it worked when you used it yesterday. You have faith that when you sit at your desk, the chair will hold your weight and not collapse under you. I could go on, but I think you get the picture. You are trusting things to function according to their design when you use them. Your faith isn't just what you believe in terms of God or whatever your beliefs are. It's a daily force that is so ingrained in your life that you don't think of it.

As a tool in your utility belt, faith can provide a foundation for your beliefs. You know what your name is. No one can convince you that your name is something different. Faith comes with a knowledge of truths that you cannot be talked out of. This is a tool that you can use when your environment or someone is trying to tell you a lie about who you are or what you can do. If your faith is grounded in God's truth, you will not be shaken when resistance tries to make you doubt your truth. You can do what God says you can do. You can be who God called you to be. You are a Superhero with a purpose that will change the world.

In *The Matrix*, Morpheus spent his life looking for the One. The Oracle prophesied that he would find him. When he found Neo, he knew he had found him. Trinity wasn't sure about Neo, but she had received a prophetic word from the Oracle. Her faith in the Oracle's words made her believe when she began to watch Neo more closely. Neo was clueless. When Morpheus explained what he believed, Neo was full of doubt and disbelief. As he learned and grew in his skills, he began to believe. By the end of the movie, he was full of faith that he was the One. He proved it by demonstrating mastery over the Matrix and changing the world.

*Solutioneering:* Yes, I made up a word to describe one of the tools in your utility belt. You know what a solution is. The suffix -eer is added to the titles of people who produce, handle, or are significantly associated with the base word. In this case, you are someone who can look at a situation and spot what's missing. You look at the current solution and generate a more complete answer to the problem. As a solutioneer, you can see solutions to fix broken systems, clarify unclear designs, and generate ideas for products the world never knew they needed. To maximize this tool, you need the constant help of Lady Wisdom and her friend Prudence. You can learn about these two powerhouses by reading Proverbs 8.

*Your "YES":* I believe your superpower is something God wants to use to make the world a better place. You are like a secret agent with projects and missions that you can accept or reject. Accepting the mission equates to you saying "YES" to God. Your "YES" is like a container filled with every tool you will need to successfully complete the mission. Remember that pasta sauce commercial with the "It's in there!" slogan? Treat your "YES" like it's that special sauce. What do you need?

- Do you need finances? It's in there!
- Do you need staffing? It's in there!
- Do you need materials? It's in there!
- Do you need wisdom, designs, creativity, strength, connections, and other resources? It's in there!

Every completed mission brings an invitation to another one. Every invitation has a fully supplied "YES." I dare you to use your "YES" to change the world!

*Empowerment:* Empowerment is a tool that you can't put a value on because when given, the recipient is the only one who can maximize its use. The definition of empowerment is the giving or delegation of power or authority. A synonym for empowerment is a blessing.

If you can't tell by now, empowerment is one of my greatest gifts. It can be yours too! Did you ever watch vintage episodes of Saturday Night Live where Hans & Franz come to "Pump [clap] you up"? Guess what? I am here to do the same thing for you! I'm not here to fluff your feathers or say what you want to hear. I am here to bring out God's best in and for your life. I'm here to speak life to the dreams you left to die along the course of your journey. I'm here to empower you with the strength to go back in and fight the good fight. I am in your corner to remind you that the fight is fixed in your favor. I am wired to observe you and see what I have that I can bless you with. How can I make an impact in your life? Whether it's knowledge, skills, testimonies, anointing, words of encouragement, wisdom, a listening ear, or a simple, "You've got this!" I am here to pump [clap] you up!

*Pause for Reflection*
I've mentioned some of the items in your utility belt. Can you think of more?

_____

_____

_____

_____

_____

**Power Up**

The tools listed in this chapter are a few of the many other possibilities. The bottom line in this chapter is this truth: YOU ARE NOT ALONE IN THIS WORLD! You have been fully equipped to accomplish incredible things. I am cheering for you. I want to know how I can help you develop your superpower. As a form of empowerment, I want to pray a blessing from the book of Numbers over your life.

"The Lord bless you, and keep you [protect you, sustain you, and guard you]; The Lord make His face shine upon you [with favor], And be gracious to you [surrounding you with lovingkindness]; The Lord lift up His countenance (face) upon you [with divine approval], And give you peace [a tranquil heart and life]."[31]

---

31 Numbers 6:24–26 AMP.

# Notes

# Chapter 9
## Using Your Superpower to Change the World

Before you hyperventilate about going public with your superpower, let's walk through your progress up to now. We can discuss what's next after I ensure we're on the same page.

In the introduction and first chapter, we started with me telling you that you are a superhero with an innate ability that is your superpower. In chapter 2, I followed that by offering suggestions to assist your search for those innate abilities. We went through a bootcamp (chapter 3), where I asked you a series of questions to help you hone your superpower through research and modeling the lives of others who have similar superpowers. If you hadn't identified your superpower yet, in chapter 4, I gave you a key to your natural ability to create. I told you how you were created in the image and likeness of the Creator of all things. After all this, I talked to you about protecting your identity and not forgetting who you are (chapter 5), learning how to partner with others to maximize the power of unity (chapter 6), how to defeat your villains (chapter 7), and finally, in the previous chapter, what tools are in your utility belt.

If you are unconvinced that you are a superhero at this point, I encourage you to put this book down for a few weeks. Pick it back up later and start over from the beginning. You may think, "Madeline, why would you tell me to stop reading your book?" My answer is timing. Some books are for different times in your life. It may not be the right time to process this information, and I want you to read it when you are ready to step into your greatness. I have books that I started and stopped because their message wasn't resonating with where I was in life. Sometime later, I picked up the same book and read it cover to cover within a few days because I was in a better headspace to understand it.

If you want to keep reading, let's keep going. I want to see your super side come out and play. This is your big, beautiful life. It should be a series of incredible adventures, innumerable learning experiences, and fulfilling victories, surrounded by a community of people who love and support you.

Using your superpower to change the world can be broken down into a big-picture plan with three major parts. Part 1 starts with you and is further divided into four practical steps, as follows:

Step 1 - Own it

Step 2 - Practice it

Step 3 - Grow and develop it

Step 4 - Maintain it

Parts 2 and 3 depend on your ability to repeat the steps and expand to wider audiences. Let's get started!

## Part 1

Changing the world with your superpower starts with you. That may seem obvious, but I want to clarify this. After determining your superpower, you must own, practice, grow, develop, and maintain it. Realize that this isn't something new to you. You have had it your whole life, and now it's time to share it with the rest of the world.

So, what does it look like to start with you? Every aspect of your superpower should be visible in your daily life before others benefit from it. Do you know the instructions flight attendants give in their safety speech? The part where, "If oxygen masks are deployed, please put on yours before helping the small children traveling with you." If you grew up churched, this goes against everything you were taught. You were taught to prefer others before yourself. (Please don't write me letters sharing scriptures that contradict what I'm telling you.) Jesus communed with His Father every morning before doing anything. He prepared for the day ahead to ensure He was able to be a blessing to the people He would encounter. When He descended the mountain, He poured out teachings, miracles, signs, and wonders. Many people were able to breathe in tough times because Jesus put His mask on first.

**Step 1 – Own it:**

I told you that I'm an encourager and your biggest cheerleader. If I follow my own advice, I should encourage and cheer for myself more than anyone else. I've had to grow into this ability because countless times I've made the error of putting others first. As a creative, I receive incredible ideas and inventions that sometimes sound impossible when I say them aloud. By now, I'm used to reminding myself of this verse from Luke, "Not one promise from God is empty of power. Nothing is impossible with God!"[32] My rule is "If I can think of it, somehow it must be possible." Prior to focusing on the promises of God, I would exhaust myself on projects for others that would encourage and exalt them or their businesses. Don't misunderstand me; this is a good thing. The problem was I put them in front of myself. Since then, I'm my biggest cheerleader first. I encourage myself so that when I hear the same encouragement from others, it's not my first time hearing it. I can wholeheartedly accept the compliment or encouragement and own it.

As an encourager, I've also sought out other encouragers to learn from their examples. A famous encourager from the Bible was King David. He talked about encouraging himself when he was in a tough situation. Read the story from 1 Samuel 30. I must encourage myself! What I've learned about encouragers is that they are everywhere. A lot of them are life coaches, mentors, teachers, managers, and all types of leaders. I watch and learn from these types of people in my life regularly. I realize that my gift, just like yours, is rich with

---

32 Luke 1:37 TPT.

newness, and I will never stop learning more about it. This is all a part of "owning it."

## Step 2 – Practice it:

I've gone from owning it to now needing to practice it in my life first. You may ask, "Madeline, what does it look like to practice encouraging yourself?" That's a great question. The answer is the mirror. Yes, I said the mirror. I stand in front of the mirror and talk to myself. Most people think talking to yourself is crazy. The truth is it's only crazy if I am telling myself lies that are self-defeating and full of doubt and disbelief. If I'm truly encouraging myself with life-giving words of truth and power, it is like medicine to me. Be advised: what others think about this practice is not important. I should give weight to what I say to myself more than what anybody else says to me or about me. Faith comes by hearing.[33] When I talk to myself, I grow in faith about the things God says about me.

Sometimes I am faced with hard challenges that appear as impassable mountains in my path. In moments like that, I remember David's fight with his giant. By now, I know how to destroy those mountains and defeat any giants in my way. I declare with my creative superpower that I am more than a conqueror and a world overcomer through the life and example of Jesus Christ.[34] I stand in the mirror and boldly proclaim who I am. If I'm not near a mirror and something pops into my head about a challenging situation I'm facing, I announce aloud what my creative words have already

---

33 Romans 10:17.
34 Romans 8:27 and John 16:33.

established: "I AM A VICTORIOUS OVERCOMER, AND ALL THINGS WORK OUT FOR MY GOOD!" If you need another example, read about the temptation of Jesus in Matthew 4:1–11.

## Step 3 – Grow and develop it:

First practicing my superpower on myself helped me grow more in confidence as the superhero I am. This growth became unnoticeable to me the more I practiced it, but other people started noticing. They would say, "Madeline, you are so encouraging and positive!" Or "how are you this happy every morning?" I really liked when I heard, "Madeline, you always see the best in people." I realized that I was beginning to display the results of my superpower without even trying.

I'm sure this has happened to you too. Have you ever started making small changes in your eating habits or added daily exercise? Maybe you started walking 30 minutes before work every day. As you did it consistently, it became easier and easier. You realized your clothes began to fit a little better, but you didn't see any major change in your reflection. One day at work, you saw someone who hasn't seen you in months, and they asked, "What's different? Have you changed your hair or started working out? You look great!" You were surprised because they noticed and none of the people who saw you daily had said anything. The gradual changes in your physiology over time are harder to spot for people who see you regularly.

Growing and developing your superpower may not have immediate physical/visual results, especially if your superpower isn't something like having the ability to leap over tall buildings or seeing through walls. The ways I grew and developed my abilities included gleaning from mentors and teachers, reading and listening to books on similar topics, putting myself in rooms where I wasn't the smartest person, studying people to find common traits, asking lots of questions, and acknowledging that the learning process never ends. I grow and develop daily.

**Step 4 – Maintain it:**

I've embraced my superpower and own it as a functioning, inseparable part of who I am. I've practiced it on myself to make it foundational to my personality. I've grown and developed it daily. Now I have the privilege of repeating that cycle nonstop.

Have you read the story in the Bible where a religious scholar asked Jesus what was the greatest commandment? It's found in a couple of places. One of them is Mark 12:28–34. To get directly to the point, I'll jump to Jesus' answer in verses 29 through 31. Jesus answered him, "The most important of all the commandments is this: 'The Lord Yahweh, our God, is one!' You are to love the Lord Yahweh, your God, with a passionate heart, from the depths of your soul, with your every thought, and with all your strength. This is the great and supreme commandment. And the second is this: 'You must love your neighbor in the same way you love yourself.' You will never find a greater commandment than these."[35]

---

35 Mark 12:29–31 TPT. Emphasis added by the author.

This is a powerful key in sharing your superpower with the world because it depends on you loving God first, then loving yourself, and then loving others with the same love you have been given by God. It is impossible for you to truly love others if you don't first love yourself. This is not a narcissistic love; this is a pure, value-filled, abundant, unselfish love. It is filled with compassion, hope, forgiveness, grace, mercy, and so many other things. Read 1 Corinthians 13. When you can receive that reckless love from God, you can pour that type of love on the world around you.

## Part 2

Since you are super within yourself, it's time to use that power to change your immediate surroundings. Now is when you look at your family and friends. Start with your spouse, your children, close friends, and family members. I started with my sisters. I reminded them what they liked to do growing up and how good they were at certain things. I told them that what they were doing as professionals allowed them limited-to-no ability to exercise their gifts. I asked them how they could start incorporating some of their gifts into the looser practices at work to see how what they are naturally good at would enhance their work. As they shared their gifts more, new opportunities opened to them. They began to gain favor with their colleagues and managers. They were considered for promotions that better fit their gifts. They have grown to a place where the amount of favor they have with their managers causes them to be first in line for company travel where they can shine even more to the company's bigger bosses.

This started as an exercise where I used my superpower of encouragement to empower someone I love. I've done the same thing with nieces and nephews as they question what's next in their lives. I LOVE blowing wind into their sails to watch them soar on new ideas and concepts they're creating. They are brilliant people, and I am privileged to partner with their transformation into the superheroes they were born to be.

I repeat the same process for close friends who are seeking answers. They are phenomenal teachers, bosses, administrators, entrepreneurs, doctors, attorneys, scientists, inventors, designers, builders, barbers, beauticians, engineers, and all other professional people. What I've found in speaking to most of them is that their superpowers are exercised after work while they are winding down for the day or when they're working on weekend projects. I encourage and empower them to do what makes them who they are: start the podcast, buy some art supplies and paint, teach some fitness classes, pull out the turntables and DJ a party, sign up for the marathon, and do what their heart has been yearning to do. I want to shake awake the sleeping superhero inside.

## Part 3

After exhausting my list of family, friends, neighbors, and colleagues, I put my gift on display for a wider audience. I take to social media and share my message on videos, posts, groups, and personal websites. I join discussions that allow me to pour encouragement into others. I speak to all the people who have had success with me helping them and depend on the power of word-of-mouth advertising to cause my message to invade every conversation. I build platforms where people can come together to share their discoveries about their superpowers with others. I write a book or a series of books for people to buy and share with others. I take myself seriously enough to become a certified mentor, life coach, and motivational speaker. I expand my exposure as I continually create new ways to encourage others to step out of the shadows and into their superhero spotlight.

This method of sharing my superpower (and yours) is a model taken from the Bible. In Acts 1, Jesus had been crucified, buried, and resurrected. He was seen all over Jerusalem by many people who could testify that He was alive. They kept asking Him about the timing of Israel's freedom and the Kingdom's restoration. He explained that God, His Father, was the only one who knew the dates. Still, it was essential that they stayed in Jerusalem until the Holy Spirit arrived to help them become witnesses to the miraculous resurrection. As witnesses, they would spread the message about Him in Jerusalem, through Judea, to the distant provinces, and even to the remotest places on earth.

As a superhero, you start with yourself and your immediate family and friends (Jerusalem). From there, you share the news about being super to the communities around you (Judea). The news becomes widespread and disperses to larger communities, even different cities in other states (distant provinces). Finally, you travel abroad to a small village in a remote country, untouched by today's society, and give each person the good news that they are superheroes (the remotest places on earth). And that, my superhero friend, is how you use your superpower to change the world.

## Power Up

Supers Rise UP! The world is looking for heroes. What people in the world don't know is that THEY are the superheroes they're looking for. Have you ever been talking on your phone as you're preparing to leave your house, but you can't find your phone? Hahaha, I know that's a crazy question, but it's a real thing. The thing you're looking for is closer than you think. Your superpower is the thing that you've been waiting for to give your life meaning and significance. Sometimes it takes another person to tell you that the phone you're looking for is in your own hand.

Be empowered to be super! I believe in you. You were made for this!

# Notes

# Chapter 10
## Going from Impossible to I'm Possible

The word impossible is defined as
1. incapable of being or of occurring
2. felt to be incapable of being done, attained, or fulfilled[36]


No superhero movie is complete without an impossible moment. If it's a good movie, there are many such moments. I'll default to *The Matrix* again to give you some examples. Remember at the beginning when Trinity had to run from the police and the agents? The first impossible thing she did was run up and around the walls. She fought her way out of the room, jumped from one building to the next, and raced to the phone booth to pick up the ringing phone just before

---

36 https://www.merriam-webster.com/dictionary/impossible

being smashed by a dump truck. That she lived through it all was impossible, and it was just the beginning of the movie. (OK. We're at the end of the book. If you still haven't watched *The Matrix* yet, I don't know what to say to you. There's probably a lesson about obedience somewhere in here.)

What about the scene where the little boy told Neo that bending the spoon with his mind is impossible because "There is no spoon." The key to bending the spoon is realizing you're bending yourself. Deep stuff, huh? Then there's the moment when Cypher has helped the agents capture Morpheus and is killing the other team members one at a time. He's talking on the phone to Trinity the whole time, gets to Neo, and says something like, "If Morpheus was right, I won't be able to pull Neo's plug. If Neo really is the One, something miraculous will have to stop me." At that exact moment, Tank gets up and shoots Cypher. Cypher unknowingly called for a miracle, and the impossible happened.

Some of the impossible moments in my life are those times when the rock moving toward me is about to squeeze me between the hard place behind me. At those moments, something supernatural happens, and I make it out. It's been happening to me my whole life. It's the moment like when we were kids, and my mom was cooking the last bit of food in the house when someone knocked on the door with bags of groceries. It was the moment when I was learning to trust God. I went to church knowing I didn't have a ride home and that He would need to speak to someone to give me a ride home. Just as I was standing there smiling and saying hi to people, a kind lady walked past me and stopped in her tracks. She looked at me and said, "Hey, do you need a ride home?" Internally, I was tripping out because of God's ability to prove Himself in my life. I said, "Yes, I do! Thank you!" When she asked where I lived, it turns out that my house was a simple stop on her way home. She not only gave me a ride home, but she offered to come and pick me up for church every week!

It's like Jesus being pushed toward a cliff by an angry crowd and walking through them.[37] It's like another time when Jesus was speaking truths that sounded blasphemous to the religious leaders. "Jesus said to them, 'I give you this eternal truth: I have existed long before Abraham was born, for I AM!' When they heard this, they picked up rocks to stone him, but Jesus concealed himself as he passed through the crowd and went away from there."[38] Did you read those words correctly? Did it say that Jesus concealed Himself and passed through the crowd? If I'm reading this with my superhero imagination, I just saw Jesus put on a cloak of invisibility and leave the room. What's your interpretation?

How many more examples of the impossible being made possible do you need? I can keep going, but I think you get the message. Let's break down the word "impossible." It starts with a commonly contracted version of the two words, "I" and "am." Those two words form a "power phrase" that defines the person who is using them. In Exodus 3, Moses

---

37 Luke 4:28–30.
38 John 8:58–59 TPT.

had an encounter with a burning bush. The voice from the bush was giving him instructions about delivering the Israelites from Egyptian bondage. When Moses asked whom he should say sent him, verses 14 and 15 are His introduction: "God replied to Moses, 'I am who I am. Say this to the people of Israel: I am has sent me to you.'15 God also said to Moses, 'Say this to the people of Israel: Yahweh, the God of your ancestors—the God of Abraham, the God of Isaac, and the God of Jacob—has sent me to you. This is my eternal name, my name to remember for all generations.'"39

There have been numerous generations since God declared His eternal name. He is still "I AM," and anyone who uses those words when introducing themselves is announcing their origin. Every positive affirmation and confession begins with "I AM." You can use this knowledge as empowerment for whenever you talk to yourself in the mirror.

I told you earlier that you are just like God, whom Jesus revealed in flesh and blood. That means we are also like Jesus who is clearly a superhero. All of this comes down to you being a superhero who possesses a minimum superpower of creativity. I have good news for you. Before Jesus was crucified, He empowered the disciples with the following words: "I tell you this timeless truth: The person who follows me in faith, believing in me, will do the same mighty miracles that I do—even greater miracles than these because I go to

---

39 Exodus 3:14–15 NLT. Emphasis added by the author.

be with my Father!"[40] If I'm using my superhero imagination, I just saw Jesus handing out superhero uniforms fully equipped with utility belts that include the same abilities He displayed, along with a Mary Poppins carpet bag full of special tricks.

I have good news for you. Regardless of how you feel about the Creator, I believe all these scriptural truths apply to you. Your simple action is that you must believe it too. Your mindset about impossible situations must shift because of these powerful words spoken by Jesus: "With people [as far as it depends on them] it is impossible, but with God all things are possible."[41] He didn't call out a group of people for whom this statement is true. There are no distinctions here: race, gender, age, religion, or any dividing factor. This means it applies to me, you, and everyone else in the world, from the newest baby born to the oldest person alive. That is an empowering and encouraging truth if you choose to believe it. You know where I stand.

I realize that I didn't finish breaking down the word impossible. The word possible is defined as
1. being within the limits of ability, capacity, or realization
2. being what may be conceived, be done, or occur according to nature, custom, or manners

---

40  John 14:12 TPT. Emphasis added by the author.
41  Matthew 19:26 AMP. Emphasis added by the author.
42  https://www.merriam-webster.com/dictionary/possible

If you put I AM and add Possible to it, you're declaring that you are <u>within the limits of ability, capacity, and realization</u>. *You are the embodiment of what can be conceived, done, or occur according to the nature, custom, or manners of the Creator of all things.*

As I'm writing this, I think I have identified another villain in the word or concept of "the impossible." You know what we have to do with villains when we find them, don't you? We must equip ourselves with the tool(s) that will defeat them. This is a fight that will be won inside of yourself first. You can use your creative ability to repeat the verse that Jesus said in Matthew 19:26. There's another great verse to add to this one; it is found in Philippians 4:13. You should go ahead and add another pocket to your utility belt with this tool.

At the time of this writing, I'm facing what most people in the world would call impossibility. This project is far beyond most people's imagination, but I believe and know that it is as easy for God to help me as it was to help Moses free the children of Israel from Egypt. I also know that God can do more for me than I can ask, think, or imagine.[42] I am also aware that the infinite God who has seen my life in totality[43] has good plans to prosper me.[44] My hope and faith are set on partnering with God to fulfill the biggest mission I've ever been given. My unconditional "YES!" has been given, and my project will be completed successfully. I hear

42 Ephesians 3:20.
43 Isaiah 46:10.
44 Jeremiah 29:11.

you asking, "Madeline, what is your project and how will we know when you've accomplished it?" My answer to you is, "You will know it when you see it because it will change the world." In the words of Bruno Mars, "Don't believe me, just watch!"

The title of this chapter is "Going from Impossible to I'm Possible." I've shared stories that refute the power of the word impossible. I've also shared the words of Jesus that you can repeat to build up your belief and confidence to defeat the idea or concepts of impossibility. My proposal to you is for you to replace the word impossible with the statement, "I'm Possible." Converting that word will empower you to stand on a negative idea and transform it into a springboard to infinite possibilities. In the words of the incomparable Audrey Hepburn, "Nothing is impossible; the word itself says, 'I'm possible!'"

## Power Up

Do you realize you're living in a world where everyone you meet has a superpower? Most people would say something like, "If everybody is super, then nobody is super." Well, most people are wrong!

We live in a world with space for everybody to be uniquely super. Your superpowers may overlap and have similarities with others', but as a unique, fearfully, and wonderfully made[45] masterpiece, how you express your powers differs. We are a world filled with a diverse variety of individual people existing on different continents. Unifying

---

45 Psalm 139:14.

in diversity, we find strength. Fixing our focus on finding, growing, developing, and sharing our superpowers with each other is what will cause the rips and tears caused by division and separation to be mended. We have a job to do. I want to do it with you and not against you. Let's be a team and change the world!

With God, all things are possible, including you! It's time for you to be the I'm Possible-minded superhero you were created to be. The creators of Buzz Lightyear coined it, but his catchphrase, "to infinity and beyond," is as prophetic as they come. All of creation is groaning for superheroes to arise. Will you do the work it takes to share your superpower? Join the I'm Possible movement and Let's Go!!

# *What's Next?*

Now that you're finished reading *Born to Be Super*, you're probably wondering if there's more. Well, of course, there's more! I have been thinking about the big picture of this project for a while. I will not leave you hanging. Let's go the distance together.

Here are some resources that will help you continue developing your superpower while connecting with others on the same journey.

Websites
BorntoBeSuper.com
Iam-possible.com

Social media page
https://www.facebook.com/Im.Possible.biz

# Born to Be Super

Look forward to:
- Blogs
- Chat sessions
- A membership option for premium content
- Monthly check-in video streams
- And more

Future Books
- Born to Be Super for Kids (with parental guides)
- Born to Be Super for Teens
- Born to Be Super for Young Adults

Future:
- After-school or special program curricula with instructor guides
- Sunday school, mission groups, and orphanage curricula with instructor guides
- Merchandise
- And much more

This is the beginning; there will be more! Stay tuned.

If you have found this book helpful, please provide a review on Amazon.

# Notes

# Notes

# Notes

# Notes

# Notes

# Notes

# Notes

# Notes

# Notes

# Notes

# Notes

# Notes

# Notes

# Notes

# Notes

# Notes

# Notes

# Notes

# Notes

# Notes

# Notes

# Notes

# Notes

# Notes

# Notes

# Notes

# Notes

# Notes

# Notes

# Notes

# Notes

# Notes

# Notes

# Notes

# Notes

# Notes

# Notes

# Notes

# Notes

# Notes

# Notes

# Notes

# Notes